From nomads to migrant
workers, people have
always looked for better
opportunities in new places.

4

12 THINGS TO KNOW ABOUT GLOBAL IMMIGRATION

BLACK RABBIT BOOKS | PRECIOUS McKENZIE

Table of Contents

Human History and Immigration
Go Hand-in-Hand

Today's news is full of stories about **immigrants**. But immigration is not new. People have always moved to different places to meet their needs. People traveled from Africa to Asia 120,000 years ago. From there, they spread to Australia, Europe, and the Americas.

Why do people move to new countries? Some reasons have stayed the same over time. People want to get away from war and violence. They leave places that lack food, water, and shelter. They want good schools and good jobs. They want the chance to make their lives better.

Some reasons for immigrating are new. Climate change is leading to more natural disasters. These cause people to leave their homes. New technology has created demand for new jobs.

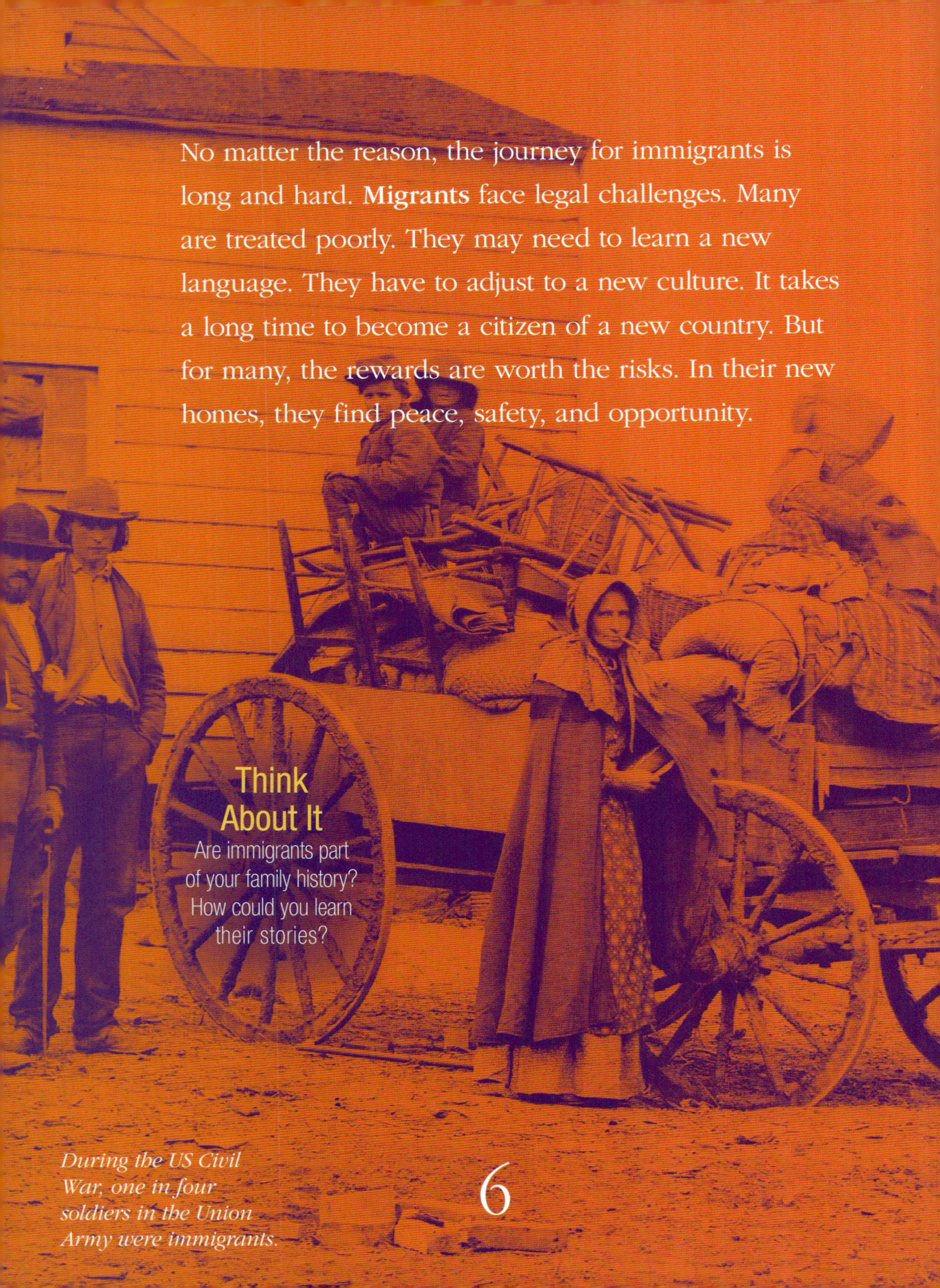

No matter the reason, the journey for immigrants is long and hard. **Migrants** face legal challenges. Many are treated poorly. They may need to learn a new language. They have to adjust to a new culture. It takes a long time to become a citizen of a new country. But for many, the rewards are worth the risks. In their new homes, they find peace, safety, and opportunity.

Many seasonal workers are immigrants, especially in the agriculture industry.

281 million People who live outside the country in which they were born.

This is about 4 percent of the world. • About 14 percent of people in the United States were born in other countries. • In 2020, 41 million migrants were under the age of 20.

Immigrants Seek Safety *and Freedom*

2

All people want to be safe. When they feel unsafe at home, many choose to leave. In 2011, war began in Syria. More than 6 million people have fled since then. In 2022, Russia invaded Ukraine. As many as 200,000 Ukrainians began to leave each day. Violence in Venezuela and the Israel-Hamas War have also **displaced** millions of people.

People also want to be free. They want to follow their own religious beliefs. Some people are **persecuted** because of their race, gender, or religion. In China, there are Muslim people called Uyghurs (WEE-gorz). They have been treated badly. Many are put in prisons. In Afghanistan, women and girls are beaten. They are forced to marry.

People who are persecuted often move to a new place. They ask the country's government for safety. Some

Minefields have made the
Ukranian countryside
very dangerous.
40 Percentage of refugees who are children.
More than 14 million refugees are under the age
of 18. • Some children migrate with their families.
Others travel alone. • Many children come from
Syria, Afghanistan, Ukraine, and South Sudan.

may seek **asylum**. If their claim is approved, they become a refugee. It can take months or years to get approved. Refugees get special protection and help. Officials may help them settle in a new country.

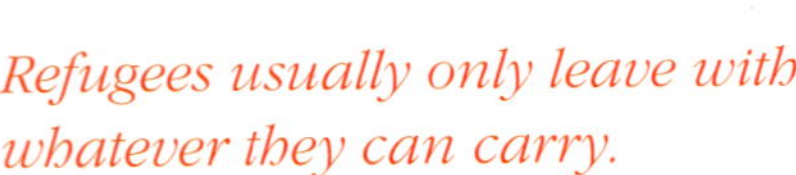

Refugees usually only leave with whatever they can carry.

A woman sits in the rubble of a house that was destroyed by war.

Natural Disasters Drive People to *New Places*

3

Natural disasters are caused by changes in the weather and environment. They can damage buildings and roads. Crops get destroyed. Power lines are knocked down. All this makes it hard to get back to normal life. A big disaster can destroy a community.

Some disasters happen suddenly, like a tornado or a hurricane. Others become worse over time, like pollution. After a disaster, diseases may spread. It can be hard to get food and water. People may have to leave their homes to find help.

Climate change is making the weather more severe. It is making environments more fragile. Big disasters will happen

1931 Year the Yangtze River flooded in China. It is the worst natural disaster ever. More than 69,000 square miles (180,000 square kilometers) flooded. • Nearly 4 million people died. • About 51 million people were injured.

more often. Communities may not have time to recover in between them.

In 2020, East Africa started to experience its worst drought in 40 years. For years, there was not enough rain. Crops and animals died. People traveled far to find food and water. The disaster created over 264,000 migrants.

In 2023, two earthquakes struck the country of Türkiye. Cities were left in ruins. Fifteen million people were harmed and left homeless. Many were Syrian refugees. They lived in flimsy shelters that did not survive.

MAICA'S STORY In 2010, a powerful earthquake shook Haiti. Maica was buried under a building for six days. Rescuers flew her to New York. She got a life-saving surgery. A charity group helped her immigrate. In her new country, Maica went to college and became a nurse.

A Changing Climate Will Increase *Immigration*

4 Climate change is warming the world. The past 10 years have been the hottest in recorded history. Scientists say that temperatures will keep rising. This will lead to more natural disasters. Storms will be bigger and sea levels will rise. Heat waves will last longer. These changes will be the hardest on poor countries. These places lack the resources for major cleanups.

As the climate changes, human behavior is changing too. Many people are seeking new homelands with more comfort and safety. The number of these "climate refugees" is growing. In the next 25 years, tens of millions of people may flee from tropical parts of the world. These areas include Latin America, South Asia, and Africa.

The Maldives is an island nation in the Indian Ocean. Its highest point is just 8 feet (2.4 meters) above sea level.

7 million

jobs that need to be filled around the world. Number of "green"

"Green" jobs reduce the effects of climate change. • They include putting up solar panels and building wind farms. • Immigrants could become "green" workers in their new countries.

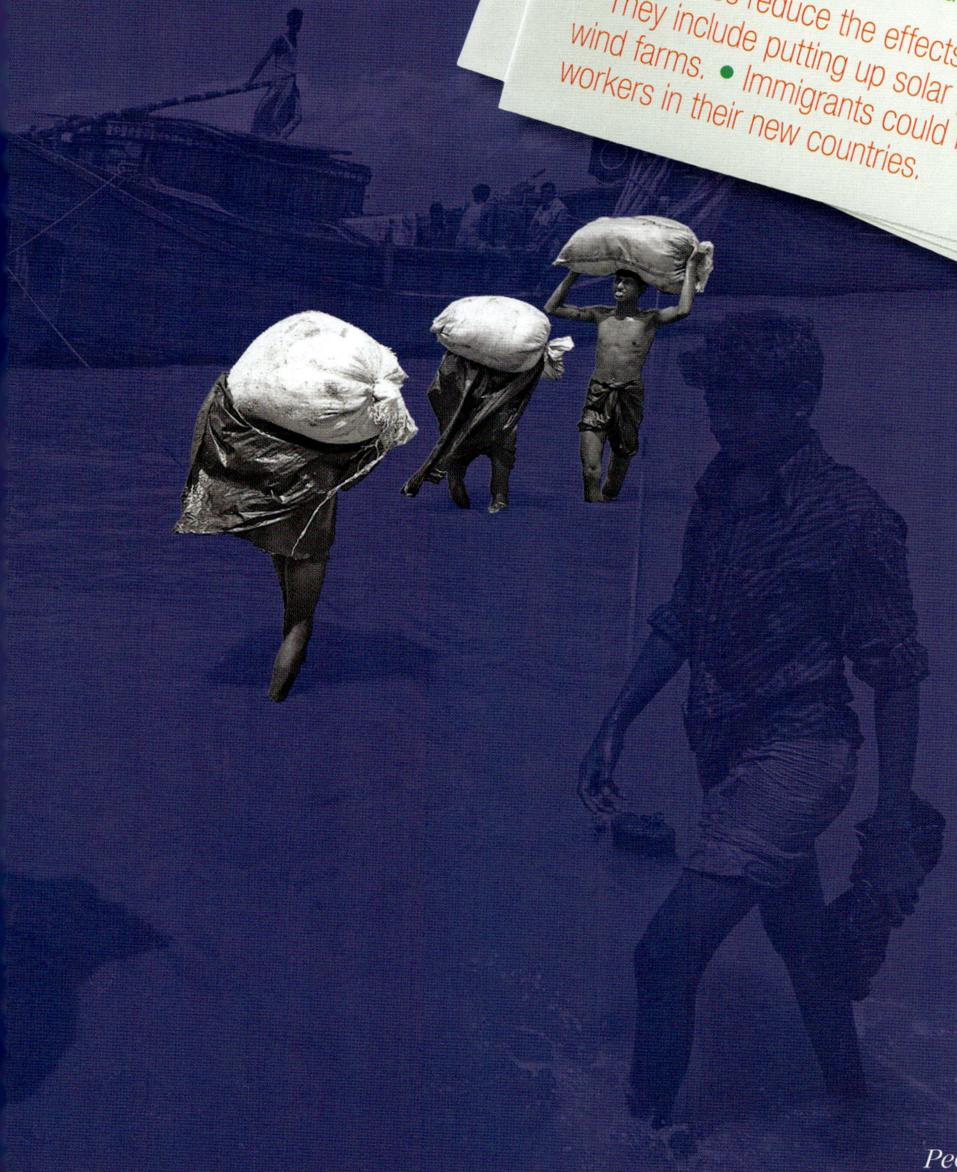

15

People carry goods to and from boats after a port disappears due to rising sea levels.

Rising water levels could sink the country's 1,200 islands. The country's people would need to go to other nations. The government of the Maldives is working on a plan.

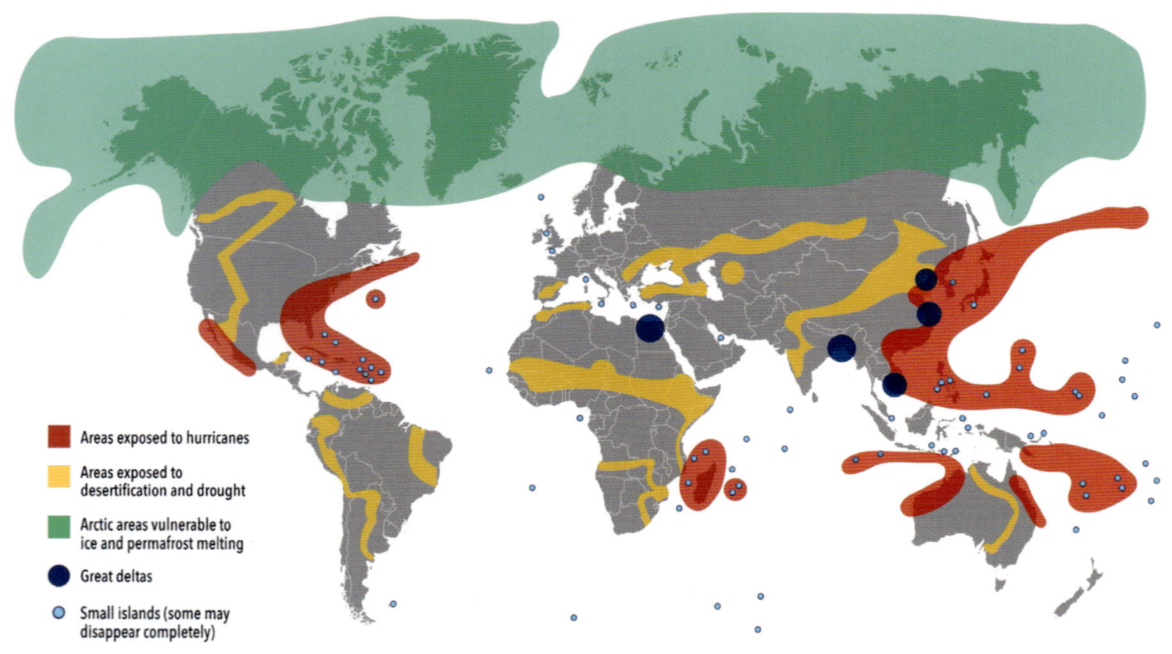

Rising sea levels will cause flooding in coastal cities.

Immigrants Hope for New *Opportunities*

There are factors that *push* immigrants away from home. These are usually bad things, like wars and disasters. There are also pull factors. These attract people to new places. These good things include health care, schools, and jobs. In some countries, most people are poor. They have few opportunities. Immigrants want to leave countries like these. They hope to improve their lives. Parents want better lives for their children.

Many immigrants want to go to nations with good public schools. Education is one of the best ways for children to have better lives. Germany has great schools. They are free all the way through college. This is a big pull factor. Nearly 40 million adults say they would like to move to Germany.

Education is a top reason people immigrate.

The promise of good jobs also attracts immigrants. Countries with stable governments and natural resources have more opportunities. They usually need more workers too. There are more jobs in countries with advanced technology. Plus, tech work is a growing field. Money is the top reason immigrants choose to come to the United States.

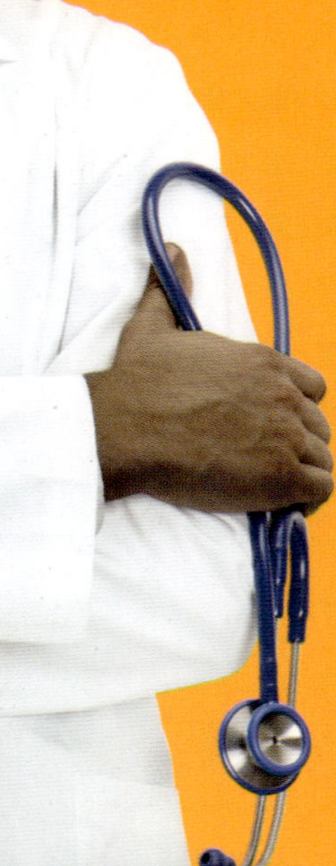

People trained in science and technology can easily find work in a new country.

KATYA'S STORY

Katya Echazarreta is from Mexico. Her family moved to California in 2002. She was seven years old. At first, she didn't speak English. School was hard. But she worked hard and learned quickly. In college, she earned a degree in engineering. She was hired by NASA. In 2022, she flew into space. She is the first Mexican-born woman to fly into space.

Katya stands in front of a mural painted in her honor in Mexico City.

Many Laws Limit *Immigration*

6

Hundreds of millions of people in the world have left their home countries. Many more want to join them. In 2021, 16 percent said they would like to live in a different nation. That's over a billion people!

Most migrants want to go to rich countries. They want to go to the United States, Germany, and the United Kingdom. Saudi Arabia and the United Arab Emirates are also popular. These nations all have immigration limits. These are set by laws. Governments worry about taking in too many immigrants. There may not be enough resources for everyone. There is fear that immigrants may take jobs from citizens. People worry that schools will get too crowded.

Limits can be hard. Some countries turn asylum seekers away. For those allowed entry, refugee status is not a guarantee. They could still be sent back home.

The law is different for those who choose to move.
The United States gives **visas**. These let people
come for a short time. Some work or go to school.
Others visit family. Australia and Canada have
a point system. People with more points have a
greater chance of getting in. Special work and
language skills earn points.

Think About It

How do you think immigration limits
affect other countries?

Visitors must apply for a visa before
visiting certain countries.

Afghan women protest with signs, demanding refugee status in India.

Undocumented Migrants *Take Risks*

7 Many migrants know they cannot enter a country legally. They may not be official refugees. Their request for asylum might be turned down. They may not be able to get a visa. But they cross the border anyway. They want a better life. They take their chances as **undocumented** immigrants.

These migrants brave great dangers. They pack onto tiny boats. They hide inside trucks. They walk through deserts and swim across rivers. In the past 10 years, about 63,000 people died or disappeared trying to enter countries illegally.

Undocumented migrants have few rights. In America, they can be reported to officials. This often happens when a person has committed a crime. Or they stayed longer than their visa allowed. They are arrested and

A family crosses a river from Mexico into the United States to seek asylum.

1,933
Length in miles (3,111 km) of the US-Mexico border.
This is the world's busiest land crossing. • It is watched by drones and US Border Patrol agents. • Thousands of people try to cross illegally every day.

held in jail. They go to a trial where a judge might rule to **deport** them. Then they have to go back to their home country.

Undocumented immigrants cannot legally hold a job. But they do important work. They build houses and fix cars. They pick crops. They take care of children and make things in factories.

Undocumented immigrants live in fear of jail and deportation.

The Path to Citizenship *Is Long*

There are many rules for legal immigrants who want to stay in a country. In the United States, they must apply for a permanent resident card. If they get a card, they can stay in the country for the rest of their lives. It can be hard to get a card. For every 1,000 applications, the United States gives out only three or four cards.

A legal immigrant can try to become a **naturalized** citizen. This happens after living in a country for a few years. First, they must fill out a form. They pay a fee and see a doctor. They may have to pass a language test. Often, there is also a test about the nation's laws and history. Then, they take an **oath** of citizenship. All these steps can take months or years.

US permanent resident cards are also called "green cards" because of their color.

Some countries do not have long waits. In Singapore, any worker can ask to become a citizen. Other countries have extra rules. In Japan, you must send a handwritten letter. You must agree to change your name. In United Arab Emirates, young men must do more than a year of community service. In Liechtenstein, you must live there for 30 years!

Department of Justice
Immigration and Naturalization Service

A Welcome to U.S.A. Citizenship

Think About It

Many immigrants feel proud to become citizens of a new country. What makes you proud of your country?

15
Number of months it usually takes to become a US citizen.

In 2023, 878,500 immigrants became naturalized US citizens. • About 88 percent of immigrants pass the US citizenship test on their first try.

Immigrants Face *Discrimination*

9

Immigrants overcome many hardships. They leave their old homes. They cross **international** borders. They take steps to become residents or citizens of a new country. But living in a new place brings even more challenges. Immigrants might not know the culture. They may not speak the common language. Daily tasks such as going to the grocery store or the doctor can be hard.

Immigrants often face **discrimination**. People may not rent an apartment to them or give them a job. Immigrants are often victims of racism and abuse. They may not know that it is against the law for others to mistreat them. They may not understand their rights.

Some people think that many immigrants are here illegally. This is false. Most immigrants come to a country because they respect its laws. They want

1 in 3 Immigrants who have been told, "Go back where you came from."

About one-third of immigrants have been insulted for speaking a different language. • Most US immigrants have faced discrimination at work. • Immigrants are often bullied at school.

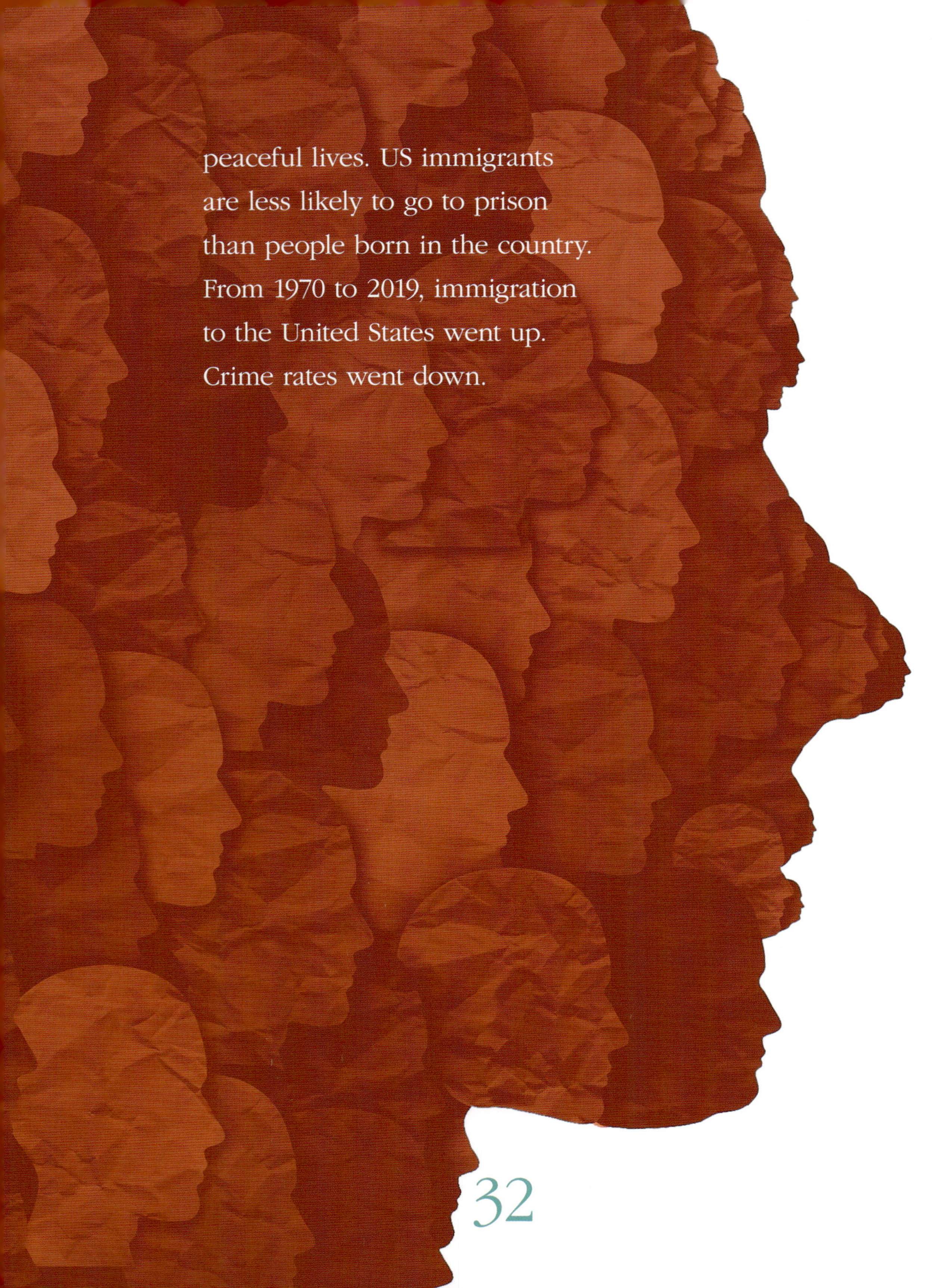

peaceful lives. US immigrants
are less likely to go to prison
than people born in the country.
From 1970 to 2019, immigration
to the United States went up.
Crime rates went down.

ISABEL'S STORY Violence in
Libya forced Isabel and her family to flee.
They used all their money to ride a boat to
Italy. One of the first Italians Isabel met was
unkind. The woman said, "Sit on the floor
and do not speak. You should kiss our hands
and say, 'thank you, Italy' because you were
poor and your country had nothing."

Countries and Organizations *Help Immigrants*

10

Immigrants need help with basic needs. They need help **assimilating** to their new homes. Many countries have programs to help. Some give language classes and job training. Canada is known for being very welcoming. It provides many services. It supports people as they build new lives. One out of every four people in Canada was born in a different country.

Many international groups help migrants. The World Health Organization (WHO) provides health care. The Red Cross helps with disaster relief. UNICEF helps children. The United Nations (UN) is important for immigrants. It has agencies that help refugees. Some agencies protect the rights of immigrants. Others give care and support. Care is important for refugees. Often, they travel long distances with very little.

4 to 7 Years it takes an immigrant child to learn a new language.
A person's accent begins to change in just a few weeks of practice. • It is easier to read and understand a new language than it is to speak and write it. • Immigrants must learn new phrases such as "It was a piece of cake."

They need clothes, food, water, and shelter. The UN also helps them find missing family members.

Small groups also play a big part. Churches and communities offer support. Individuals can even **sponsor** new immigrants. The groups donate furniture and give car rides. They help with finding jobs. Some groups go to the airport to cheer for immigrants when they first arrive. It is a warm welcome to the new country.

Think About It What do you think immigrants want and need most in their new countries? How could you help?

The UN uses planes to move people and supplies to countries around the world.

Immigration Strengthens Families *and Cultures*

Immigration spreads people all over the world. But it also brings families and communities together. Many immigrants go to countries where they already have family. It is easier to enter that country legally. Family members can sponsor new residents.

Once immigrants get jobs, many send back **remittances**. This money goes to family members they left behind. It helps them afford the things they need. As much as $800 billion each year is sent to other nations. These include India, China, and Mexico.

Immigrants tend to choose countries where other people from their homelands have settled. This forms a support system. It helps the new immigrants succeed. Over time, neighborhoods and cities attract many people from one part of the world. These communities

enrich the local culture. They bring new types of food, music, and art.

In their new countries, immigrants learn about new holidays and customs. They often combine new and old traditions. In the United States, immigrants might celebrate Thanksgiving with a turkey dinner that includes tamales, curry, or pierogis.

58 Percentage of legal US immigrants who come to join family.

Family members may be husbands, wives, children, parents, brothers, or sisters. • Most come from Mexico, India, and China. • The most popular states for immigrants are Florida, Texas, and New Jersey.

Above: Red lanterns in Hong Kong

Below: Indian classical dancer

Above: Carnival of Venice in Italy

Below: Running with the bulls in Spain

Immigrants Make Countries *Richer*

12

Some people think immigrants are bad for a country's **economy**. They believe immigrants take jobs away from citizens. They think that immigrants drain money from the government. These ideas are false. Undocumented immigrants and permanent residents cannot get most government aid. Many immigrants start businesses that create new jobs. Nearly all immigrants work and pay taxes.

Many rich nations do not have enough workers. Their citizens are getting older. Their populations are going down. Immigrants make these countries stronger. They fill important jobs. Many do heavy labor that no one else wants to do. In the past 20 years, the number of US workers has gone up. Much of this growth is due to immigrants and their children.

Construction work is one type of job an new immigrant might do.
Think About It
What could make your community
better for immigrants?

Skilled workers are wanted around the world. Countries really need computer programmers and engineers. They need doctors, nurses, and teachers. Some nations have programs to attract immigrants with college degrees and special skills. The United Kingdom gives a 2-year visa to top college graduates from around the world. A special visa in New Zealand includes training for immigrants who want to start businesses. Immigration helps fuel the economy. Despite the hardships immigrants face, the risk is often worth the rewards. Many immigrants find the better life that they are seeking.

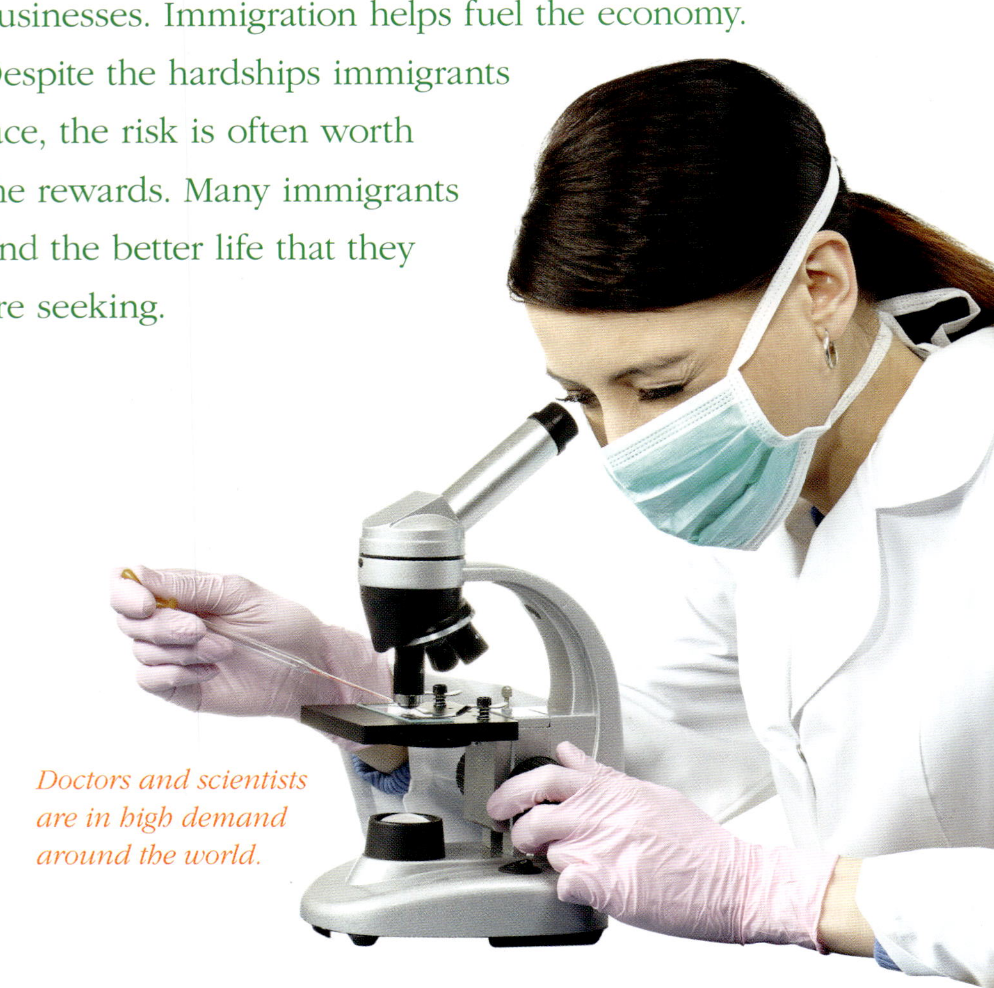

Doctors and scientists are in high demand around the world.

An orchard field boss shows an migrant worker how to pick pears.

Fact

- Ellis Island is a famous US immigration station. It opened in 1892 in New York Harbor. Annie Moore was first to pass through. She was a teenage immigrant from Ireland. In the following 62 years, more than 12 million immigrants arrived at Ellis Island. The station closed in 1954. Today, you can visit the island. There is a museum to learn about immigration back then.

- Millions of students travel to a different country to go to college. The number gets bigger each year. International students often come from China, India, Vietnam, and France. The United States, Australia, United Kingdom, Germany, and Russia host the most students.

Sheet

- There are 350 different languages spoken in the United States. More than 40 million people in the US speak Spanish. About 4 million speak a Chinese language. The next most popular languages are Tagalog, Vietnamese, and Arabic. Many immigrants are eager to learn English. It is the world's most popular language. About 3 out of every 4 English speakers learned it as a second language.

- War began in 2022 when Russia invaded Ukraine. Many Ukrainians needed to escape. The European Union (EU) acted quickly. Its government passed laws to give temporary protection to Ukrainian citizens. Anyone fleeing the war would have a right to housing, work, education, and medical care. Nearly 4 million people from Ukraine fled to the EU.

Glossary

assimilating
Fully becoming part of a new culture or group.

asylum
A place of refuge, shelter, and protection; sanctuary.

deport
To lawfully force someone to leave a country.

discrimination
Prejudice or unfair behavior against someone based on differences in things like age, race, or gender.

economy
A country's system of buying and selling; all the money that flows through a country.

immigrant
A person who leaves their old country and settles in a new one.

international
Involving more than one country.

migrant
A person who has left their home and is traveling to a new place.

naturalized
Becoming a citizen of a country.

oath
A promise.

persecuted
Continuously treated cruelly or unfairly, especially because of a person's ideas or beliefs.

refugee
A person who is forced to leave a country because of war or for religious or political reasons.

remittance
An amount of money that is sent as a payment for something.

undocumented
Not having the official documents needed to enter, live in, or work in a country legally.

visa
An official mark or stamp on a passport that allows someone to enter or leave a country, usually for a particular reason.

For More Information

Books

Anderson, Robert Tuesley. *Rights for Migrants and Refugees: How You Can Make a Difference.* Tuscon, AZ: Brown Bear Books, 2024.

Spengler, Kremena. *The Immigrant Experience.* Mankato, MN: Creative Education and Creative Paperbacks, 2025.

Sutton, Patricia. *Immigration.* Lake Elmo, MN: Focus Readers, 2024.

Websites

Nick News: Kids, Immigration, and Equality
www.youtube.com/watch?v=Xo-aHleRBRo

Scholastic: Meet Young Immigrants
teacher.scholastic.com/activities/immigration/
young_immigrants/index.html

UNICEF: Migration
data.unicef.org/topic/child-migration-and-displacement/
migration/

Index

Library of Congress Cataloging-in-Publication Data Names: McKenzie, Precious, 1975- author. | Title: 12 things to know about global immigration / by Precious McKenzie. | Description: Mankato, MN: Black Rabbit Books, 2025. | Series: Today's headlines | Includes bibliographical references and index. | Ages 9–13 | Grades 4–6 | Identifiers: LCCN 2024026478 | ISBN 9781645823858 (library binding) | ISBN 9781645824077 (paperback) | ISBN 9781645824299 (ebook) | Subjects: LCSH: Emigration and immigration—Juvenile literature. | Classification: LCC JV6035 .M3185 2025 | DDC 325/.1—dc23/eng/20240708 | LC record available at https://lccn.loc.gov/2024026478